Rabbits and Hares

Rabbits and Hares

by Robert Whitehead

← A FIRST BOOK →

FRANKLIN WATTS | NEW YORK | LONDON | 1977

Franklin Watts Limited,
26 Albemarle Street,
London, W.1.

Diagrams by Peter Stanziale
Cover design by Terry Fehr

Photographs courtesy of: Australian Information Service: pp. 20, 37;
National Institutes of Health: p. viii; New York Public Library Picture Col-
lection: p. 7; New York Zoological Society: pp. 41, 48, 56 (top right *and*
bottom); U.S. Department of Agriculture: pp. 15, 47, 51, 55, 56 (top
left), 59; U.S. Fish and Wildlife Service, photo by W. P. Taylor: p. 23,
photo by O. J. White: p. 24; from the motion picture *Get to Know Your
Rabbit* courtesy of Warner Bros. Inc. copyright © 1972: p. 16.

Contents

Rabbits and Hares

Rabbits and Hares: Heroes or Enemies?

Of the 3,500 species of mammals on earth to-day, one group or Order, called *Lagomorpha*, consists of two families, the *Leporodae* (rabbits and hares) and the *Ochotonidae* (pikas). It seems that the ancestors of these animals first appeared shortly after the age of dinosaurs. At that time it became safe for mammals to come out of hiding to search for food during the day.

Rabbits and hares are the most familiar creatures. They are often thought of as charming, well-behaved creatures of field and forest. With their baby faces, snub noses, and soft, cuddly bodies, they seem carefree, fun-loving, and cheerful. Small wonder that in so many tales told to children the rabbit or hare plays the part of the lovable, daring hero. And rabbits and hares seem to have an almost unbelievable ability to escape from their enemies. Because of this they are also often thought of as being tricky, sly, or clever, such as in the Uncle Remus tales of Br'er Rabbit (who always outwits the dangerous Br'er Fox).

J.A.S

But believe it or not, rabbits and hares were, and still are, believed by many peoples of the world to be evil or to represent the darker, more shadowy side of life. The rabbits' habit of eating only the choicest leaves in a vegetable garden makes them wasteful destroyers of crops. The speed with which hares can escape from fleet-footed pursuers may have led others to consider rabbits tricksters, possessed of evil magic.

What are the members of this Order really like? Well, all have furry bodies (all mammals have hair covering at least part of their skin) with long ears and fluffy tails. They live on most continents and on some islands of the world, in fields and woods.

Because they all look so much alike, they are often mistaken for one another. Basically only their body shapes and sizes and some of their habits set them apart. All of them, however, follow similar life styles. They must all make homes, find food, bring forth young, control their numbers, and work out defences against their enemies.

Up to mischief again, Br'er Rabbit fools Br'er Fox and gets him to carry him on his back. Joel Chandler Harris was the creator of the *Uncle Remus* tales.

For thousands of years now, mankind has been in close contact with their family. Rabbits and hares have been hunted by many people throughout history. Other people have chosen to rear some of the various kinds instead. We have learned to use rabbits and hares for food, clothing, and laboratory experiments. Those who rear rabbits in garden hutches or rabbitries have had to learn also how to house, feed, and care for the animals properly, as well as how to select the best type of rabbit for the purpose it is being kept.

Rabbits and hares have also shared in the history, legends, and superstitions of a number of cultures, including our own. They have even influenced our language and geography.

Much, then, has been said about rabbits and hares, good and bad. It is up to you to decide whether they are really tricksters or heroes, clowns or mischievous wanderers and destroyers, or simply creatures of the wild trying to live out their lives the way they know best.

Rabbits and Hares
in History

By studying fossils (traces, prints, or remains of plant or animal life preserved in rock), scientists can tell that rabbits and hares have been around for about 30 million years. It is hardly surprising, then, that they have played a part in the culture, legends, and superstitions of many civilizations.

SOME FACTS

The first rabbits probably came from Africa. They then appear to have gone to Spain, where scientists have found cave paintings of rabbits dating back to the Stone Age. After that they seem to have spread quickly throughout Europe and Asia.

More than eight thousand years ago, the Egyptians trained hawks and salukis (smooth-coated heavy hunting dogs) to work together to hunt rabbits and hares. In this sport, called **coursing,** the hawk would track the rabbit from the air while the saluki followed it on the ground. When ready, the hawk would strike down the prey, and the saluki would hold it until the hunters arrived.

Rabbits played a part in the ancient civilizations of China and the Middle East. The Chinese used rabbits in religious ceremonies over two thousand years ago. In Turkey, a giant statue of a sphinx standing on two stone rabbits was built about 1500 B.C. The sphinx was supposed to represent the god Horus, who guarded temples and tombs.

Rabbits were used for more practical purposes, too. The Romans liked to hunt and rear rabbits for food. Later, during medieval times, many monasteries set up their own rabbit gardens. These were plots of ground on which rabbits were reared for eventual use in the kitchen.

SOME LEGENDS

Throughout history, rabbits and hares have been included in stories and legends from all over the world. Some of the tales were meant to be taken seriously. Some were told merely to entertain. Here are a few of the more interesting ones:

Easter Bunny. The story of the Easter Bunny of the Christian tradition goes back to a pre-Christian Teutonic (north European) legend. The rabbit was once supposed to have been a bird. It was changed to a rabbit by the fertility goddess Ostara, or Eastre

John Tenniel, illustrator of Lewis Carroll's
Alice's Adventures in Wonderland,
here shows the March Hare with
Alice, the Mad Hatter, and the Dormouse
at the Mad Tea Party.

Rabbits have always been
widely hunted for food and sport.
This is a hunting scene on a
rabbit warren in the sixteenth century.

(from whom the name *Easter* comes). The rabbit thanked Eastre by laying brightly coloured eggs each spring for the (Easter) festival given in her honour.

Great Hare. The Algonquian Indian tribes in Canada, New England, and New York State (U.S.A.) had a legend about the Great Hare Michabo. Michabo rebuilt the world after the Great Flood. He used a small piece of soil given him by the muskrat. He then shot his arrows into the soil, and the arrows became trees. By studying the spider's web, Michabo invented the art of knitting nets for fishing. Later, the Great Hare married a mouse. From this union were born the various races that people the earth today.

Hare and the tortoise. Over two thousand years ago the Greek storyteller Aesop told a fable about a race between a hare and a tortoise. The hare got off to an early lead. The tortoise went on in his slow, steady way. Soon the hare was so far ahead that he decided to take a nap. While he slept, the tortoise passed him and won the race. The moral of the story is, of course, that slow and steady wins the race.

In an African version of the fable, the story takes quite a different turn. A tortoise challenges a hare to a race. The tortoise then places his relatives along the raceway. All the tortoises look alike to the running hare. No matter how fast the hare runs, the tortoise always seems to be ahead of him. Tricked, the hare gives up and the tortoise wins.

Harelip. In an African Bushman legend, the hare is a messenger of the moon. Because the hare tells lies, the moon hits the hare in the mouth and splits its lip. This gives the creature its harelip.

Holy rabbit. Among some North American Indians, the rabbit was a holy animal. It was believed that the rabbit burrowed into the soil and freed the first human from the underworld of the devil.

SOME SUPERSTITIONS

People all over the world have always been very superstitious about rabbits and hares. To some, rabbits have meant good luck. To many others, they have meant bad luck. Here are a few of the most popular of these beliefs.

Hare's path. It is said to be bad luck to cross a hare's path when going on a journey. It is also bad luck for a bride and groom to have a hare cross in front of the wedding procession. And if a hare crossed the path of a woman expecting a baby, the baby was mistakenly believed to have been born with a harelip.

Hare signals. A hare running down the main street of a town means there will be a bad fire. To dream of a hare means the dreamer has enemies. Or it means that death is coming to someone in the dreamer's family.

Rabbit chants. If a person wants good luck or a gift, the first thing he or she should say on the first day of the approaching month is "rabbits" or "white rabbits" three times. Before going to bed on the last night of that month, the person is supposed to say "hares" or "black rabbits." If the chants get switched around or said at the wrong time, bad luck will follow.

Rabbit's foot. The left hind foot of a rabbit, taken into a churchyard at midnight when the moon is full, will protect its owner from evil. To carry a hare's foot is generally considered lucky — and keeps away rheumatism, a disease of the muscles or joints.

Rabbit shooting. In some cultures the people believe it to be unwise to shoot a black rabbit. Dead people, they think, often come back to earth as black rabbits.

White rabbits, on the other hand, were once suspected of being witches. This is because it was believed that a witch could easily change herself into a white rabbit. These witch-rabbits supposedly stole the milk from cows and sheep lying in the fields. They could be shot only with silver bullets. If one was shot, it was thought that the wound would later appear on a local person known to be a witch.

3

Humans,
Rabbits, and Hares

IN THE LABORATORY

Great numbers of rabbits have been used for medical research and other experimental work in laboratories because they are plentiful and easy to handle. A woman who is thought to be expecting a baby may be given a **rabbit test.** A sample of the woman's urine is injected into an adult female rabbit. If a special hormone, or substance produced by the body, is present in the woman's urine, some of the tiny sacs in the rabbit's ovary will burst open. This confirms that the woman is pregnant.

A person bitten by an animal that has rabies, a disease that destroys the nerve cells of warm-blooded animals, is given injections of vaccine daily for 14 days or longer. The vaccine is prepared in the bodies of rabbits. It can relieve the effects of the disease.

Rabbits have also been used in testing the germs of tuberculosis, syphilis, and allergies, and in testing the effects of newly developed drugs.

GEOGRAPHY

People have shown great fondness for naming places after rabbits. In California and Colorado alone, more than 75 streams are named Rabbit Creek. Rabbit Ear Mountain in Colorado was so named because it looked like a rabbit's ear. Conejos (KO-nay-ohs), the Spanish word for rabbits, is the name of a river in Colorado. Place names in Britain include Coneysthorpe (Yorks), Coney Weston (Suffolk), Coney Island (Clare), and the Rabbit Islands (Sutherland).

FOOD AND FUR

Hares and rabbits are an important source of protein, a substance people need in order to live and grow. They are caught in traps or shot by hunters. Wild hares and rabbits are often roasted and eaten like chicken. Their flesh is delicious in meat pies, too. The rabbit was introduced to Britain from Europe during the thirteenth century. It was prized for its food and fur, and strictly protected. Poaching rabbits was a serious crime.

Rabbit fur is used for stuffing mattresses and sofas and for making clothes. The long silky hair of the Angora rabbit is spun into a soft, warm yarn used to make sweaters. Rabbitskins are important in making gloves, hats, gelatin (a substance used in making jelly), and jujubes (gummy sweets). It takes about fifty rabbits to make twelve felt hats. Eskimos make leggings, socks, mittens, and blankets from the fur and skins of hares.

LANGUAGE

Another way in which the rabbit and hare influences our lives is through our language, shown by some of our common sayings and slang expressions.

Harebrained: someone who is foolish or wild.

Buckrabbit start: a fast, jerky start made by the driver of a car.

Mad as a March hare: Someone who leaps and jumps about crazily. This saying comes from the leaping and jumping of the male hare during the March mating season. Male hares kick, jump, and box with their forepaws to drive other males away from the females.

For use in making clothing, the fur
of the Angora rabbit is removed
by electric shears. This fur can be
blue, black, greyish-brown, or white.

Pull a rabbit out of a hat: give an answer when it seems impossible to do so.

Rabbit ears: an indoor television antenna with two aerials.

Rabbit food: a salad made with leafy vegetables.

Rabbit punch: a short, sharp punch on the back of the neck. A rabbit will deliver a kick like this to another rabbit that is annoying it.

The Polish rabbit is a toy-sized rabbit often called the "Little Aristocrat." It is the rabbit used in magic hat tricks. It has tiny ears, bold eyes, and a shiny white coat and usually weighs about 1 kilo.

The Rabbit Family

Rabbits, hares, and pikas all belong to the scientific Order *Lagomorpha* (pronounced lag-ow-MOR-fuh), meaning "form of a hare." Rabbits and hares look so much alike that some breeds of hare have often been misnamed rabbits and some breeds of rabbits have often been misnamed hares. For example, in the U.S.A. jackrabbits and snowshoe rabbits are hares and Belgian hares are rabbits.

Lagomorphs are found in most parts of the world. However, there are no members of the rabbit family in certain regions of the Middle East and South America, and on most islands, with the exception of a few in the Atlantic, Pacific, and Antarctic oceans. They live in all sorts of habitats: fields, forests, marshes, prairies, rocky slopes, open country, shrub-grown areas, tundra, and woods.

Most members of the Lagomorphs have short tails — the pika's tail is very short. The fur is long, soft, and fine in pikas. But

EUROPEAN HARE

ASIAN PIKA

JACKRABBIT HARE PIKA AMERICAN PIKA

ANGORA (DOMESTIC)

EASTERN COTTONTAIL

KONYNEN (EUROPEAN WILD) RABBIT COTTONTAIL LITTLE IDAHO RABBIT

THE RABBIT FAMILY.

People have taken wild rabbits to many
parts of the world where they had not
formerly bred. Wild European rabbits,
like the one shown here, were taken
to Australia in 1859. Finding no natural
enemies there, the rabbits overbred
and are now considered a national pest.

it runs from coarse to thick and soft in rabbits and hares.

Wild European rabbits and rabbits found in pet shops are **true rabbits.** A true rabbit is one that digs or occupies a burrow. The wild rabbit's scientific name comes from a combination of the ancient Latin and Greek words *Oryctolagus cuniculus* (o-RIK-to-lag-us kiu-NIK-you-lus), meaning "burrowing hares." A rabbit was not always called a rabbit. At one time the animal was known as a *coney* or *cony* (KO-nee), from an early Latin word meaning "rabbit" or "burrowing."

There are about five distinct species of wild rabbits.

Bristly rabbit. The bristly rabbit lives in the southern foothills of the Himalayan Mountains. It is named for its coarse outer hair.

European rabbit. This rabbit lives in Europe, North Africa, North America, Asia, Australia, and New Zealand. All pet rabbits are varieties of European rabbits. So are those raised in cages for fur or meat.

Red rock rabbit. This rabbit lives in South Africa. When frightened, it lets loose a startling series of loud screams as it races for its rocky den.

Liukiu rabbit. This rabbit is found on the Liukiu Islands, south of Japan. It has unusually long claws.

Sumatra short-eared rabbit. The rump and tail of this Asian rabbit are bright red.

Hares. Hares are not true rabbits, as they do not dig burrows or live in holes in the ground. They get their name from the Old English word *hasu*, meaning "grey." Hares are bigger than rabbits; they have longer ears and legs and larger hind feet. They run rapidly and for greater distances than rabbits. About every ten years, for some unknown reason, the hare population drops. And, surprisingly, hares warn each other of danger by grinding their teeth together and thumping on the ground with their hind feet.

There are about 25 species of hares. Here are a few.

Arctic hare. Also known as the blue, white, or mountain hare, this animal digs for shelter beneath the Arctic snow. Arctic hares have long hair all over their bodies, even on the soles of their feet. They wear white coats all year round in the far north. During the summer, in Canada and Newfoundland, Arctic hares lose their white fur and grow brown fur in its place. The mountain hare in Scotland also changes colour.

Jackrabbit. This hare of the western part of the United States is named for the resemblance of its ears to those of a jackass. The antelope or white-sided jackrabbit owes its name to its ability to dodge back and forth, causing patches of white fur on its belly to swing to either side of its body. The reflection of the sun on the white fur is believed to be a danger signal flashed to nearby hares.

The jackrabbit, shown here, normally runs at
a speed of 48–56 kph. A frightened
hare may reach a speed of up to 72 kph.

A young pigmy rabbit. The Idaho pigmy is the
smallest cottontail in the United States. It is the only rabbit
of the cottontail family to build its own warren.

Snowshoe rabbit. Long hairs on its big feet give this hare its name. In northern Europe, its cousins are called Alpine or varying hares. The name varying hares comes from the hare's ability to change its colour from season to season.

Cottontails belong to a group of North and South American animals scientifically named *Sylvilagus* (sil-vi-LAG-us), meaning "forest hare." Because they do not dig burrows, they are not true rabbits. There is a riddle about the animal's popular name of cottontail: Why does a rabbit have a shiny nose? Answer: Because its powder puff is at the other end. The answer calls attention to the ball of fur on the creature's tail, from which it earns its name. A few of the 13 species of North and South American cottontails are:

Eastern cottontail. This is the most widely found cottontail, appearing in Canada, Mexico, and the United States. Depending on where it lives, it may be called Florida cottontail, Rocky Mountain cottontail, Audubon cottontail (western United States), brush rabbit (Pacific coast), or forest rabbit (South America).

Swamp rabbit. The southwestern United States is the home of the marsh rabbit. This rabbit is comfortable in water because it swims well.

Volcano rabbit. This tiny, tailless rabbit lives on volcanoes in Mexico. It trots like a dog and whistles like a pika.

Pikas look like rabbits and hares. They are, however, a one-of-a-kind family. Since they do not burrow, they are not true rabbits. Pikas were given their popular name by the Mongolian people of northern Asia. The pika's scientific family name is *Ochotonidae* (ok-o-TON-i-dee), meaning "members of the family of pika."

Pikas are small furry animals that live in the Rocky Mountains of North America and on the steppes and mountains of Asia.

With short ears that look very much like those of a guinea pig, the pika is about 17 centimetres long, with a tail less than 2.5 centimetres in length. Its coat is greyish-brown on the back, and white or light brown on the belly.

The pika is also called a conie, cony, little chief hare, mouse hare, rock rabbit, calling hare, or whistling hare. The names "calling hare" and "whistling hare" come from its habit of sitting up watchfully, constantly making a loud bleating or whistling note. This sound may give warning of approaching danger. Or it may keep the pika in touch with others in the colony.

Pikas live among loose rock on mountainsides. There they take shelter from their chief enemies — the fox, weasel, marten, and hawk. They spend their days eating green plants, like moss and lichen. Since pikas do not hibernate (sleep through winter), they spend some time stacking plants in the sun to dry. The dried plants are later stored among the rocks for the long, cold winter.

Rabbits and Hares, Inside and Out

RABBITS

Adult wild rabbits may grow 38 to 45 centimetres long and weigh up to 2 kilos. **Does** (females) are usually larger than **bucks** (males). Wild rabbits have soft, thick greyish-brown fur. Their fluffy tails are 5 centimetres long.

To stay alive, rabbits depend on their ears and a keen sense of smell. A rabbit's ears are 5 to 10 centimetres long and work like antennas. They can move together or one at a time and can pick up faint sounds from far away. A rabbit sitting up on its hind legs and twitching its nose is smelling. The nostrils flick open, and sensing pads inside pick up scents in the air. This helps the rabbit find food. It also helps a rabbit identify other rabbits and living creatures.

A rabbit's eyes are on the sides of its head. Because of this it can see objects behind or to the side better than in front. Its large, widespread eyes also help it see over long distances and in the dark. But rabbits see everything in black and white only. And they do not see in sharp detail, as humans do.

Rabbits have two kinds of teeth: very sharp **incisors** for cutting and **molars** for grinding. The molars are in the back of the mouth. The incisors are in front. Since the incisor teeth never stop growing, rabbits must constantly gnaw on plants to keep them worn down. If they don't, they will not be able to eat properly and will starve. Between the molars and the incisors there is a wide gap, or **diastema** (dy-a-STEE-muh), very much like the gap of a horse's jaw in which the bit rests.

Further, rabbits must move their jaws from side to side in order to chew properly. A rabbit's lower jaw is narrower than its upper jaw. Because of this, there is no way the upper and lower molars can meet at the same time. This means the rabbit has to line up its lower and upper molars on one side to chew awhile. Then it rolls the food over to the other side, shifts the jaw to line up the molars, and chews some more.

A rabbit has a deep slit in its upper lip, called a **harelip.** The harelip exposes the upper incisors even when the mouth is closed. It prevents dirt from getting into the mouth while the chisel-like teeth cut into grain stalks and niches in bark to get every available bit of food.

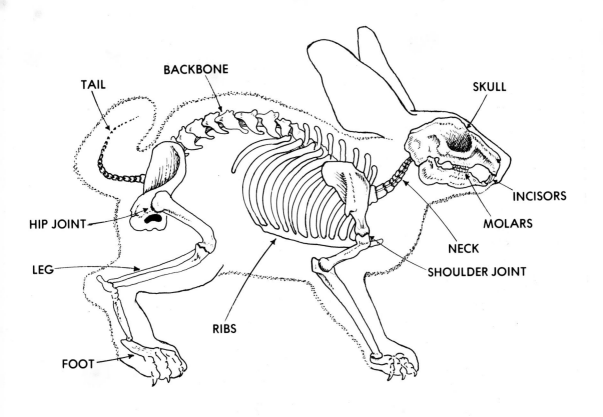

TAIL

BACKBONE

SKULL

HIP JOINT

INCISORS

MOLARS

LEG

NECK

SHOULDER JOINT

RIBS

FOOT

THE BODY OF A RABBIT.

Beneath the jaws of a rabbit are glands that secrete a colourless fluid. This fluid flows out of its mouth and down its chin as the rabbit pushes its chin along the ground. The scent of the fluid marks for a rabbit the boundaries of its territory. This action, called **chinning,** is used mainly by the bucks. Does, not as concerned with territory marking as males, secrete less fluid. In fact, if a doe has newborn young, chinning might let her enemies know the whereabouts of the nest.

A rabbit or hare will fight to defend its territory against others of its kind. The defender grazes slowly toward an unwanted rabbit, nibbling grass and seeming not to care. Suddenly, it hops towards the enemy with a curious stiff-legged gait. Its white tail is raised. Now the defender moves in a circle around the enemy. This shows its broadside and white belly, suggesting the defender is larger than it really is. The biting and kicking battle ends with the defeated rabbit or hare leaving the scene.

Most other four-legged animals walk or run — not so a rabbit. Its hind legs are longer and stronger than its front legs. This makes the rabbit able to bound along, balancing on its front legs and pushing itself forward with powerful thrusts of its hind legs. When chased, a rabbit can hop as fast as 24 km an hour. Both hind feet hit the ground at the same time but land *in front* of the forepaws. A rabbit's feet, with their sharp claws, are also useful for digging and fighting.

For grooming, a rabbit cleans its coat by licking the pads

of its forepaws. This covers the pads with saliva. Then both pads are pressed down over the sides of the face. Next come the ears. The rabbit pulls them down and rubs them clean. The fur on the body and feet is last. If patches of fur are torn from any part of the rabbit's body, new fur soon grows in.

HARES

Hares are often mistaken for rabbits. But hares are larger and longer, weighing between 2¾ and 6¾ kilos and measuring up to 70 centimetres. Males, or jacks, are about ½ kilo heavier than females. The head of a hare is longer and narrower than the head of a rabbit. Rabbits have short, rounded ears. The ears of a hare are tapered and may reach 20 centimetres in length—almost one-third of its total body length. Depending upon where they live, hares have brown, dull-yellow, grey, or white fur. Their short, bushy white tails are easy to see when they run.

A hare's coat has two layers. Close to the skin is the dense, woolly white underfur. Growing out beyond this is an outer coat of guard hairs. These two coats of fur help to keep the hare's body warm and dry as it lies out in the fields in all kinds of weather.

The soles of the hare's big feet are covered with coarse hair. These "hair shoes" prevent the northern hares from slipping on the ice. They also enable hares to bound along on top of the snow without falling through. The southern hares can race swiftly

FRONT FEET

HIND FEET

When a hare is in full flight, its hind feet
strike the ground ahead of
its forepaws. The forepaws are
spread apart, the hind feet close together.

through swamps and across sand, bounding along on top of the crusted or loose soil without losing speed.

When resting, a hare sits with body, head, and neck drawn together in a ball. All four feet are gathered underneath but planted in the ground for a quick start. Some resting time is spent grooming. The hare vigorously scratches and combs its fur, using the long claws on its hind feet. In what is a safety measure, each hind leg and foot is extended far forward for cleaning. The hare then does not have to turn its head and spoil its line of sight.

The hare's ability to burst instantly out of a relaxed sitting position into top speed is startling. It can also dodge bewilderingly at full speed. Over a short distance, the hare can outrun a coyote, fox, lynx, weasel, or wolf. When chased, the hare prefers to confuse its enemy by running a zigzag course uphill.

A hare is also a top-notch long jumper. It can cover ground in leaps of 4.5 to 6 metres. Between these long jumps, a hare makes three or four short jumps about 2 metres long. When closely followed by an enemy, the hare digs in its toes and runs low to the ground with less of a bounding motion. High jumping is common during courtship. If a male is about to catch up with a female, the female may suddenly bound upward. She will make a half turn while in the air, and, on hitting the ground, start running in the opposite direction. Meanwhile the male has passed underneath the female!

Ordinarily the running leap of a hare is no more than a few feet off the ground. But if chased, the fourth or fifth bound may reach over a metre high. This "spy" hop depends upon the height of the bushes and grass. In some cases it also depends on the kind of hare. Jackrabbits use it at all times. But hares living in snow would fall through the top layer if they pushed down too hard to gain any height.

6

A Way of Life

The life of a rabbit or hare is spent doing four main things: finding food, making a home, raising young, and avoiding enemies. To do these things well, rabbits, particularly the wild European rabbits, live in groups. Being "social" is a way of surviving. The ordinary **warren** (underground burrow) is occupied by about 20 rabbits. However, warrens that are linked together by tunnels may hold 60 young (called **kittens**), 10 does, and 3 or 4 bucks.

Hares are not generally social animals. They do not seem to enjoy each other's company and, except for a few brief moments during mating, have little to do with one another. Even **leverets** (baby hares) can survive and be on their own when they are just over two weeks old. A large number of hares — as many as 5,000 in 260 hectares (1 square mile) — are not a social gathering. They are simply 5,000 individual hares attracted to a good feeding ground.

However, rabbits and hares do "talk" to their own kind. They send out signals of danger by drumming with their hind feet, making faint groaning sounds. When frightened or injured, they let out loud, shrill screams. Hares also make warning noises by grinding their teeth together. Female hares call their young to nurse with a snorting grunt.

FOOD-FINDER

Most rabbits and hares feed at dawn and dusk. They like leafy plants like burdock, clover, marigold, primrose, and sorrel. If very hungry, they will nibble stinging nettle and sour-tasting campion. During the winter the animals eat twigs, roots, bark, berries, and the fruits of bushes and trees. Usually farmers don't like wild rabbits and hares. The animals too often destroy growing sprouts of beans, lettuce, peas, and other vegetables, or gnaw at the bark of fruit trees.

Rabbits and hares get a lot from the food they eat. There are four reasons for this. First, a rabbit has a long digestive tract. This means food has plenty of time to be broken down and used by the body before it is disposd of. Second, a rabbit has a fold in its intestine called the **caecum** (SEE-kum). This holds bacteria that break down food even further for digestion. Third, rabbits and

**A gathering at dusk of wild European
rabbits around a waterhole in Australia.**

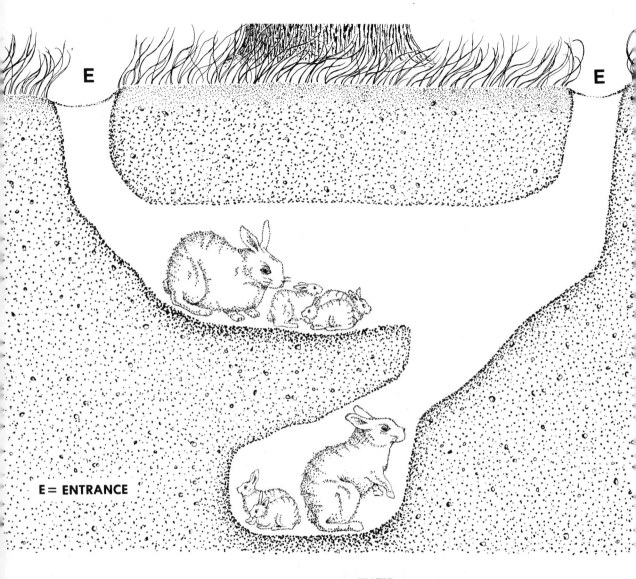

E

E

E = ENTRANCE

**DOES AND THEIR
KITTENS IN A WARREN.**

hares eat some of their food twice. Undigested food passes out of the body in the form of soft, moist, membrane-covered droppings, which they eat. This may sound revolting, but it's very practical for them. The bacteria in the droppings provide extra vitamins and proteins. Fourth, rabbits and hares regurgitate (throw up) balls of partly digested food. These balls, or **castings,** are then chewed and swallowed again. This helps the animals to get all possible nourishment out of things they eat. Pet rabbits do this, as well as wild rabbits and hares.

HOMEMAKER

Wild European rabbits usually live in a warren they have dug in a hillside. Sometimes, though, they will move into burrows that have been abandoned by badgers, prairie dogs, skunks, or woodchucks. Cottontails and hares live in sunken places in the grass called **forms.** A form is a nest where the animal's weight has pushed down the grass.

It is only the female rabbit that will take the trouble actually to build a warren. She first cuts into the soil with her forepaws. Then she piles up the dirt between her hind legs. Next she backs out of the hole, dragging the dirt with her. At the entrance, the doe kicks her hind legs and flings the soil backward under her tail. Small mounds of dirt outside the entrance are smoothed as she pushes the dirt with her chest. A finished warren has many tunnels, entrances, and exits. It also has separate areas for a number of does and their young, and a resting place for other rabbits.

PARENTHOOD: RABBITS

A doe carries her young inside her body for 26 to 30 days before giving birth. She has four to six offspring at a time. No matter what the weather, a wild European rabbit about to give birth shelters in a burrow, or **stop,** away from the main tunnel. In fair weather or foul weather, a female cottontail scrapes out a shallow nest on top of the ground. Then she lines the nest and covers the newborn kittens with soft grass and fur pulled from her belly with her teeth. This enables the kittens to feed more easily. (Like all other mammals, does nourish their young by milk produced in the mammary glands.) The covering of grass and fur is also used to hide the babies and keep them warm while the mother is gone from the nest during the day. She seals it as she leaves. At night the doe returns to the nest to care for her young.

When first born, rabbit kittens cannot see or hear and have no fur. They weigh about 56 grammes. By the time they are 10 days old, however, they can both see and hear and their weight has more than doubled. Further, they have developed a coat of soft fur.

A doe rarely cares for her young for more than four weeks.

Baby cottontails protected in their nest.

This is because she will mate again within two days after giving birth to a litter. On the average, a doe has five litters — roughly 25 kittens — in one season. The kittens of her first litter may make her a grandmother in the same year. It has been estimated that one pair of adult rabbits can have 13 million descendants in three years! A rabbit named Chewer actually fathered 36,772 offspring in his lifetime.

Before letting her kittens go, the doe trains them to run from humans, other ground animals, and birds. When the doe stamps her hind foot on the ground and raises her white scut (tail), the kittens run and hide in the grass or burrow. Young males learn to box and to chin. Young females learn to dig warrens or make nests.

Young rabbits enjoy one another's company. But the day comes when they must separate and make a life for themselves. Since the female gives birth to a new litter about every 30 days during the mating season, the young rabbits must begin to look out for themselves in a month's time. Young bucks wander far and wide during their first year of life. They have no mates to keep them near a nest or warren. Young does can breed at five months of age. They also don't usually settle too far from the nest of their birth.

When a young buck nears one year of age, he feels an urge to mate. But he must invade the territory of an older male and fight to get a doe. The young male will circle, then attack the older buck, sinking his teeth into the older buck's neck, head, and hind legs. Fur and flesh will fly. If the young male wins, the older buck backs off. The young male has won a dry warren or form with one or more does. If he loses he must retreat to an empty burrow or lie out at night in a far corner of a field, alone. Fights take place during the height of the mating season. The mating season runs from January through September for wild rabbits.

If a female rabbit does not want to mate with the new buck, she will try to get away from him. She may even kick at him, or strike at him with her forepaws. When attracted to the buck, the doe will lie on her side, exposing the white fur of her belly. She will permit the buck to lick her face, ears, neck, and fur. Or the two may sit calmly facing each other.

A buck and a doe jump, run, and "dance" about before mating. The doe flicks her tail while she leaps about. She squats down and lifts her hindquarters. Her forelegs and breast are pressed to the ground. The buck stands with his body and hind legs across the hindquarters of the doe. With rapid thrusting motions by the buck the mating is completed. The buck has placed his sperm (male sex cells) inside the female's body.

PARENTHOOD: HARES

The main breeding season for hares runs from early spring to late summer.

About 36 to 42 days after mating, the jill (female) prepares a nest by digging out a shallow round bowl in the thick grass, between 10 and 20 cm across. She then lines it with fur that the jill pulls out of her own coat. Some jills do not build a nest. The jill stops wherever she happens to be, rises on her hind legs, and drops (gives birth to) the leverets. Then the mother tears open the membrane covering the baby and eats the skinlike tissue. By the time the leveret's head and forepaws are exposed, the newborn hare has begun to struggle to reach its mother's breast. As soon as the baby begins to nurse, the jill finishes removing the leveret from its birth sac. She then licks her baby dry. All the young are born within half an hour.

A female hare may have up to 10 young in each litter. Many, however, bear only 2 to 4 at a time. The newborn hares weigh between 56 and 112 grammes. They are fully covered with very fine brown fur just over a centimetre long. They can walk and even hop soon after the mother has licked them dry. At one week they have almost doubled in weight.

Young hares do not mate until they are about a year old. Only about one-third of newborn hares reach their first birthday. Fifteen out of a hundred reach the age of two. Two in a hundred reach the age of five years. Most are killed by bad weather or enemies.

POPULATION CONTROL

Rabbits and hares have the ability to stop themselves from giving birth. Kittens forming inside a doe's body can be **reabsorbed** (made a part of her body again). This process takes about three days and usually happens by the fifteenth day of pregnancy. After that time, all the embryos (unborn kittens) have disappeared into the doe's body system. We don't really know what causes rabbits and hares to do this. But reabsorption seems to happen (1) during very cold winters, (2) when there are too many rabbits in a colony, (3) when the bucks are bothering the does, or (4) when there is a shortage of food.

ENEMIES

People are the greatest enemies of rabbits and hares. Every year hunters shoot millions for sport and food. Farmers kill thousands by running over them with farm machines, poisoning them with gas and pesticides, and catching them in traps.

Eagles, buzzards, hawks, owls, and large birds prey on rabbits and hares. The golden eagle and the large sea eagles can fly away with an adult rabbit or hare gripped in its talons, or claws. Small buzzards, hawks, and owls do the same with kittens. Dead rabbits and hares are eaten by crows, jays, magpies, and ravens.

Rabbits and hares have a great many animal enemies in addition to humans and birds. Among the best known of these are the ferret, bobcat, coyote, dog, fox, house cat, marten, skunk, snake, wild boar, wolf, and wolverine. In Europe, trained ferrets — members of the weasel family — are sent into warrens to hunt rabbits for their masters. If it believes that it will soon be attacked by a bobcat, coyote, fox, or wolf, a hare will race across an open field, dodging and changing course like a flash of lightning.

Nature also kills off a large number of rabbits and hares. Thousands starve each year. This lack of food can be caused by rabbits and hares overgrazing the land. Flash floods drown rabbits in their warrens and forms. Hares can die in minutes from "shock disease," an illness brought on by violent exercise or fright. A disease called **myxomatosis** (mik-suh-muh-TOE-sis) has killed millions of wild rabbits in Australia and Europe. Mosquitoes and fleas carry the virus to healthy rabbits. The rabbits become blind and deaf, their heads swell, and they eventually die.

DEFENCES

Rabbits and hares are not helpless against their enemies. Camouflage (natural body or fur colouring that hides something in a particular environment) makes them hard to find. Their ability to sit perfectly still, then, is often as useful as their speed, though they are quick and hard to catch. Their sight is not good. But the keen,

This snowshoe rabbit is almost completely
hidden in the snow, thanks to its white fur.

twitching nose and excellent hearing give warning of trouble. Their big ears twist this way and that. When danger is near, a rabbit or hare will stamp its hind feet to sound an alarm that warns others of the danger. It will also squeal or scream. The rustling of a rabbit or hare in a bush or tall grass is another danger signal. But as species, rabbits and hares are protected because they have so many offspring. There is safety in numbers.

A white-tailed jackrabbit changing from a summer coat of brown fur . . . to a winter coat of white fur. This is the way the jackrabbit can keep its camouflage.

Want to Raise a Rabbit?

Few wild rabbits and hares live long in captivity. They do not like to be caged. Also, they can get a disease called **tularemia** (rabbit fever), which makes the animals and humans who handle them very sick.

Tame rabbits, on the other hand, make delightful pets.

HOUSING

You can buy a **rabbit hutch** (cage) at a pet store. The hutch should be at least .60 metre high, .60 metre wide, and 1.2–2 metres long. The 1.2-metre size is comfortable for one rabbit. The 2-metre size, however, is better for rearing a family of rabbits.

With proper care and housing, a pair of rabbits
may reproduce for at least 4 to 6 years. Shown
above is an inexpensive two-section hutch, quite
suitable to the needs of the rabbit family living in it.

Or you can, if you like, make a hutch. The best kind is built with the four sides, floor, and ceiling lined with galvanized wire. The corner supports and mid-supports are made of solid wood posts, and the slanted roof of wooden slats.

In spring, summer, and early autumn, put the hutch outdoors in a shady place. Rabbits like plenty of fresh air. Hang the hutch from a tree limb with heavy wire or rope. Or you can place it on a table that is raised and has a sliding waste tray beneath it. This allows waste matter to fall through the wire. It also keeps the rabbit from trying to dig out, which would be the case if the cage is placed on the ground. Lastly it ensures that the hutch will not be flooded during a storm. During rain it is best, of course, to move the hutch to shelter.

Rabbits can also be kept indoors. In winter the hutch must be moved indoors to a sun-warmed shed or put in a well-lit utility room or garage. Placing the hutch on some kind of raised platform will protect the rabbits from draughts. A sliding tray, like a baking sheet, can be put under the hutch. It will catch the waste matter. The tray rests on top of the platform, but stands free of the bottom of the hutch so that it can be easily pulled out. Tip the hutch slightly to the rear to insert and remove the tray. Spreading a layer of cat litter on the tray will help keep down odour. Hay or straw should also be given for bedding. The rabbits will build a nest with some of the straw. But the tray and hutch should be cleaned thoroughly twice a week.

FEEDING

Pet rabbits eat pellets, barley, oats, and wheat. You can also give them some ~~apple~~, cabbage, carrot, clover, dandelion, grass, ~~lettuce~~, pear, potato, and turnip as a special treat. Rabbits should have small amounts of fresh hay to eat every night. Hay aids the rabbit's digestion. Biting the hard hay stalks also helps wear down the front teeth. A salt block to nibble on can be bought at a pet shop.

Do not overfeed your rabbit. Give it only as much food as it will eat in half an hour. Overfeeding makes a rabbit fat and lazy. Being overweight places a strain on its heart. It also shortens its life.

A rabbit needs fresh, clean water daily. You can buy water bottles with gravity tubes at your pet shop. The bottle should be hung on the outside of the hutch, with the tube reaching inside.

Choosing a Rabbit

Your choice of a breed of rabbit to keep will be determined largely by your reason for keeping rabbits — for fur, for show, as pets, or for food. To help you decide, a few breeds are described.

The **Angora** is a beautiful rabbit that looks like a heap of loose snow. It is an excellent show rabbit, weighing from 2 to 3.6

kilos. Every three months an Angora grows 112 grammes of new, soft, strong fur. The fur, or wool, is valuable in making sweaters.

Champagne d'Argent is a breed that was named after a province (county) in France. It has been kept there for over a hundred years. The rabbit has a dark, slate-blue undercoat and silver guard hairs. The babies are black, but their fur lightens to silver as they grow.

The **Checkered Giant** is mainly white in colour with checkerboard-like markings in black or blue. It is in demand both as a show and fur animal. The rabbit was first raised in Germany. Its best weight is in the 5–7-kilo range.

The Belgian hare (below) is a popular show rabbit. It can take a stand-up position, like a begging dog. Its ideal weight is 3.5 kilos. In colour it is chestnut, reddish, or tan. The average weight of the Champagne d'Argent (above) is 4.5 kilos. Its fur is highly prized by the makers of fur clothing.

The **Chinchilla** comes in three kinds: giant (5 to 6 kilos), standard (3 to 4 kilos), and American (4.5 to 5 kilos). The American chinchilla is highly prized for its grey surface fur, deep blue-grey underfur, and white belly.

The **Dutch rabbit** was first raised in Holland. It is the most popular of all show rabbits. A streak of white runs over its shoulder, under the neck, and over the front legs and hind feet.

The **Flemish Giant** is a very large rabbit with a broad chest. It reaches a top weight of 9 kilos, although its ideal weight is 5 kilos. A hutch 2 metres long is needed to keep this rabbit. This is an excellent show rabbit, with its grey or sandy fur.

Above left: the Chinchilla rabbit. Below: the Dutch rabbit. Its guard hairs range in colour from black or blue to chocolate or tortoise. Its ideal weight can vary from 1.35 to 2.7 kilos. Above right: the Flemish Giant.

The so-called **New Zealand rabbit** is black, reddish, or white. It actually first came from America. It is the most popular rabbit in the United States and is in demand for its meat. Garment makers also like to use its fur because it takes dye well. It is also a fine laboratory animal and weighs from 4.5 to 5 kilos.

Right: the Lopear has very long, hanging ears. It is known for its large head and arched (mandolin) back. Its ideal weight is 4.5 kilos.

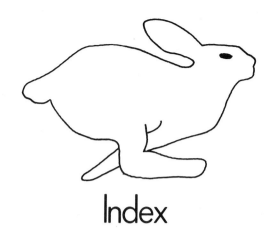

Index